The Storm

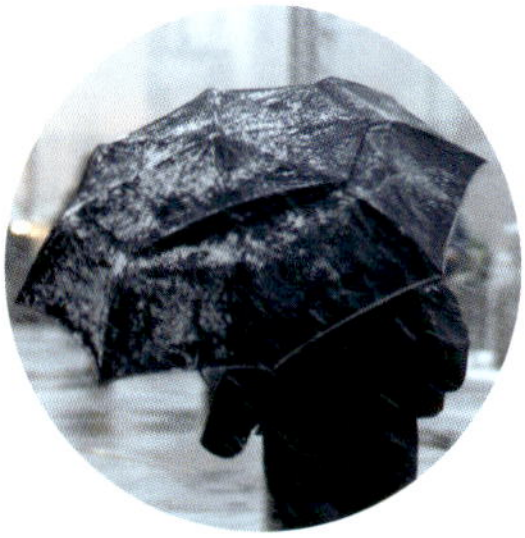

Written by
Stephen Rickard

Ransom

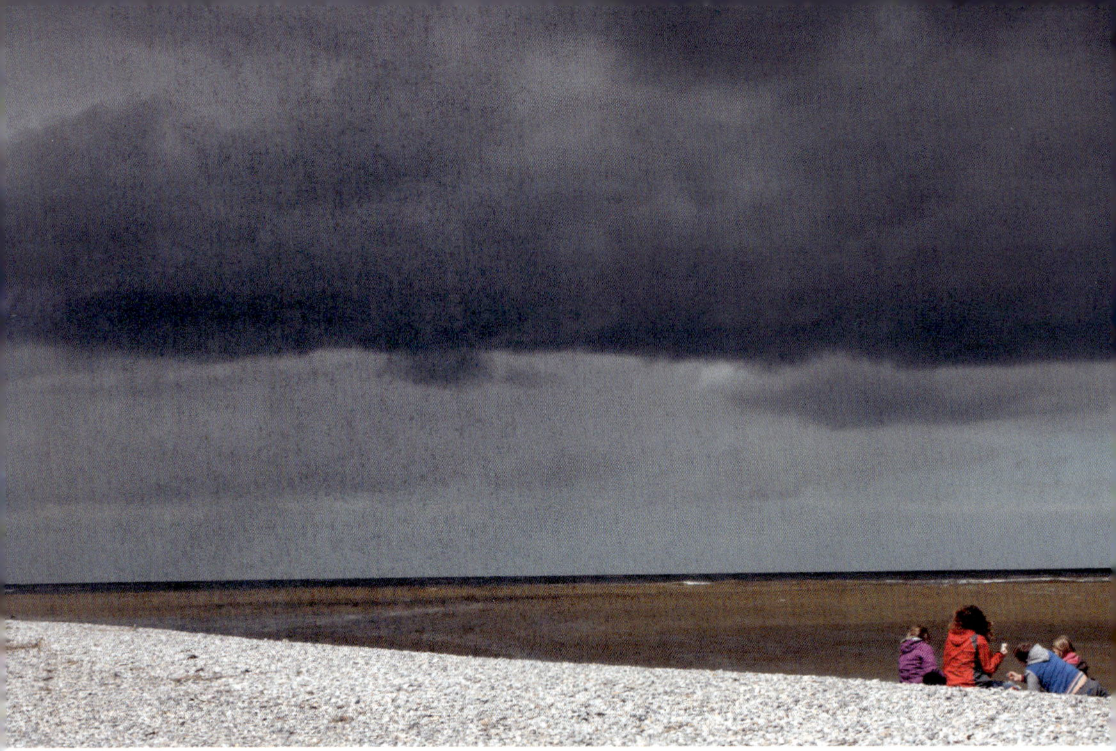

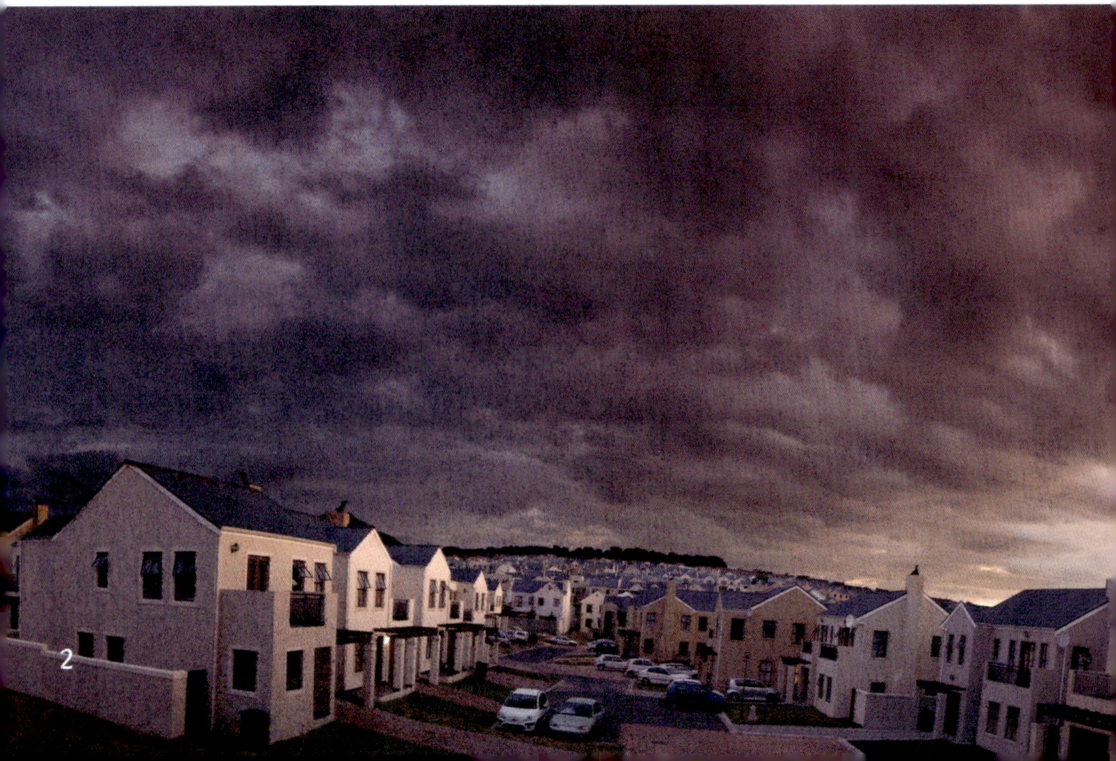

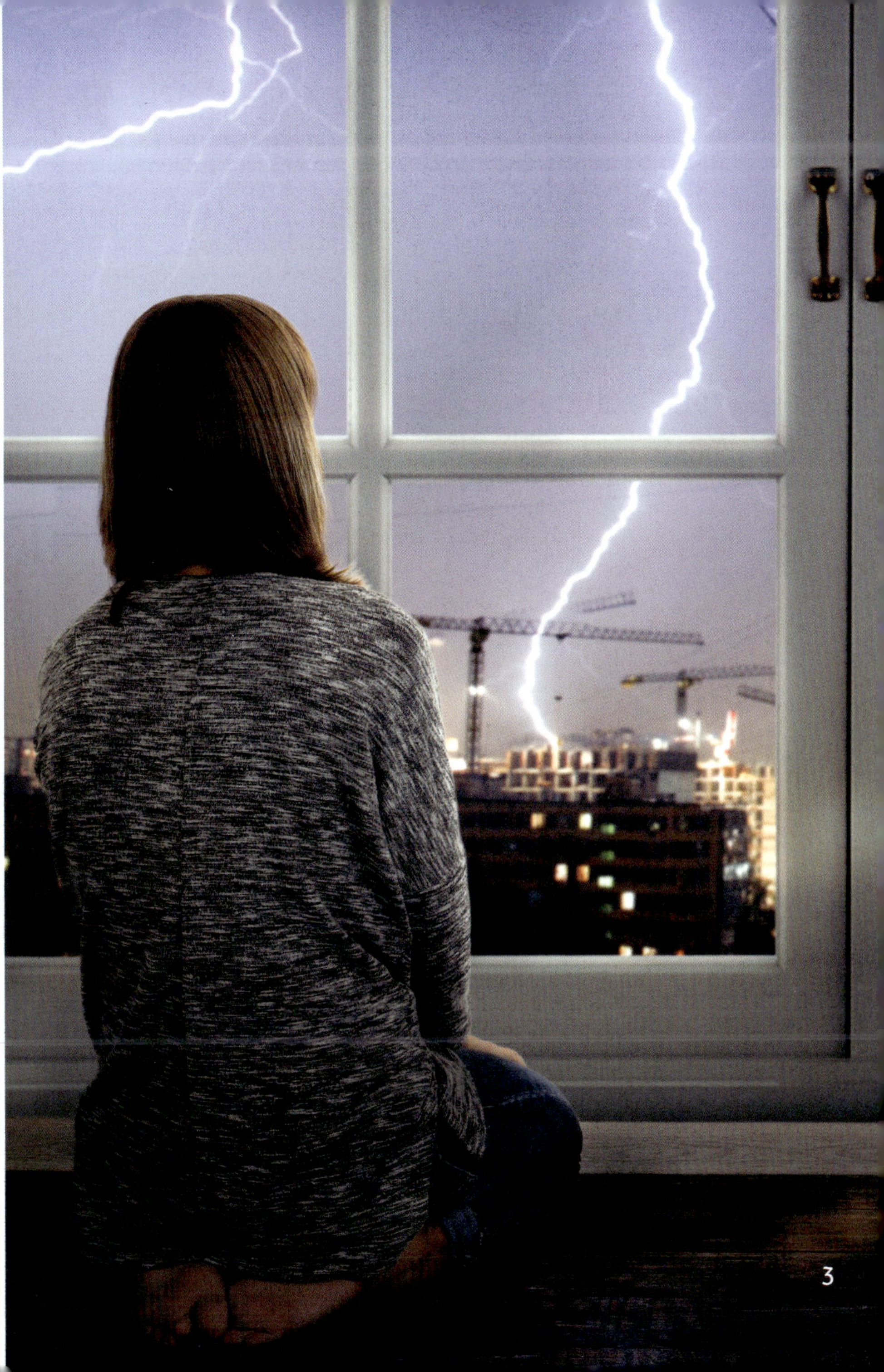

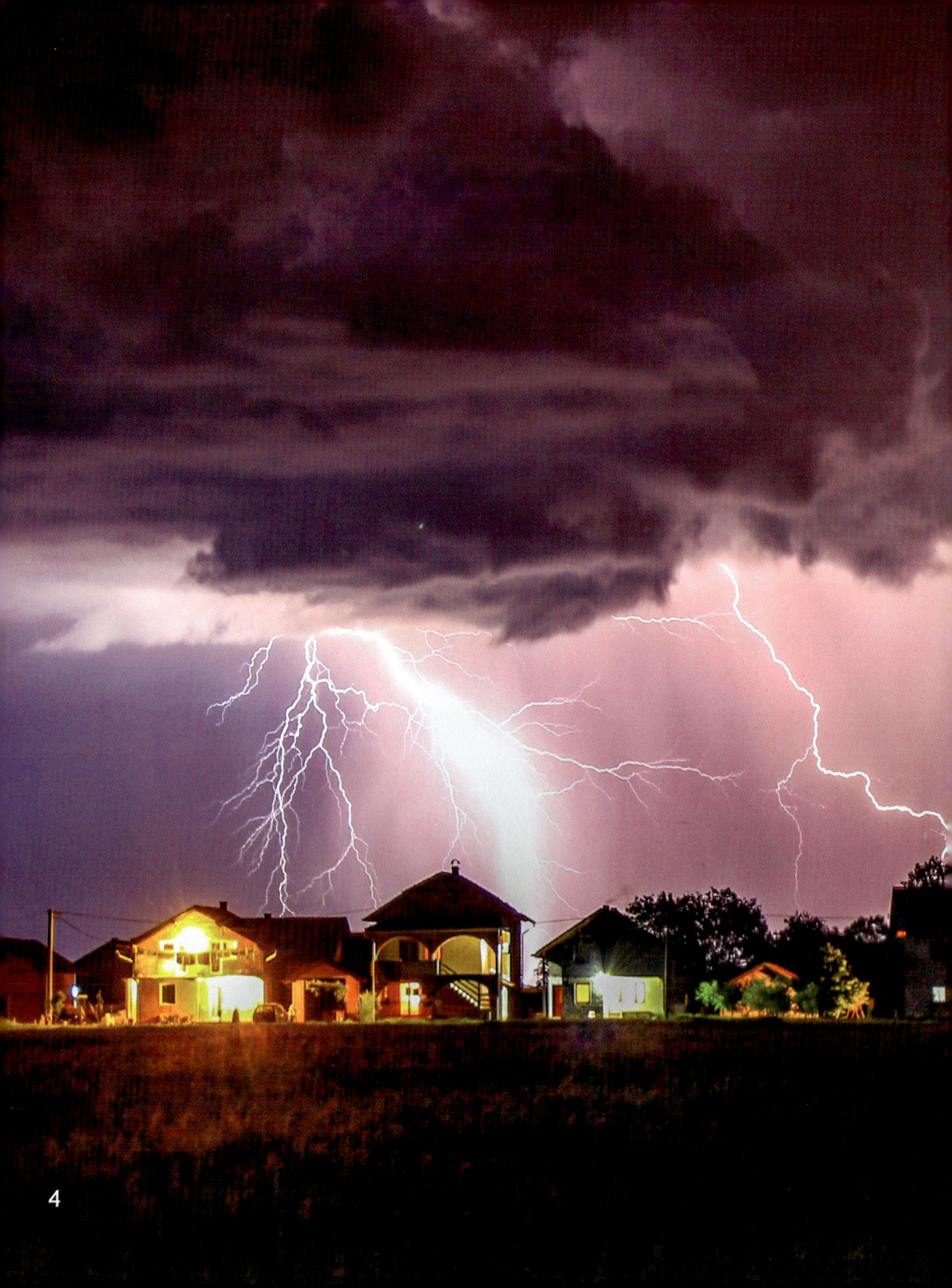

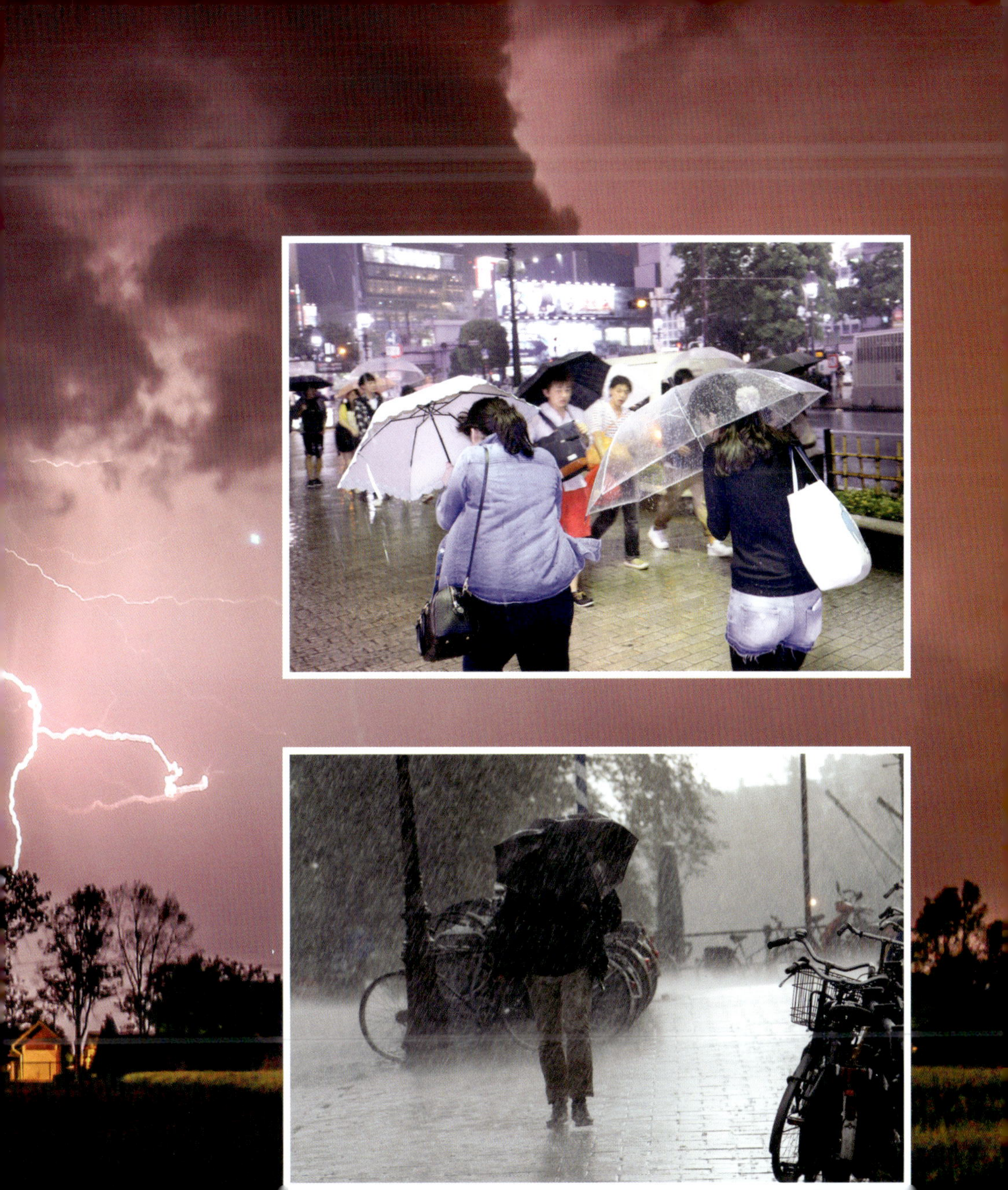

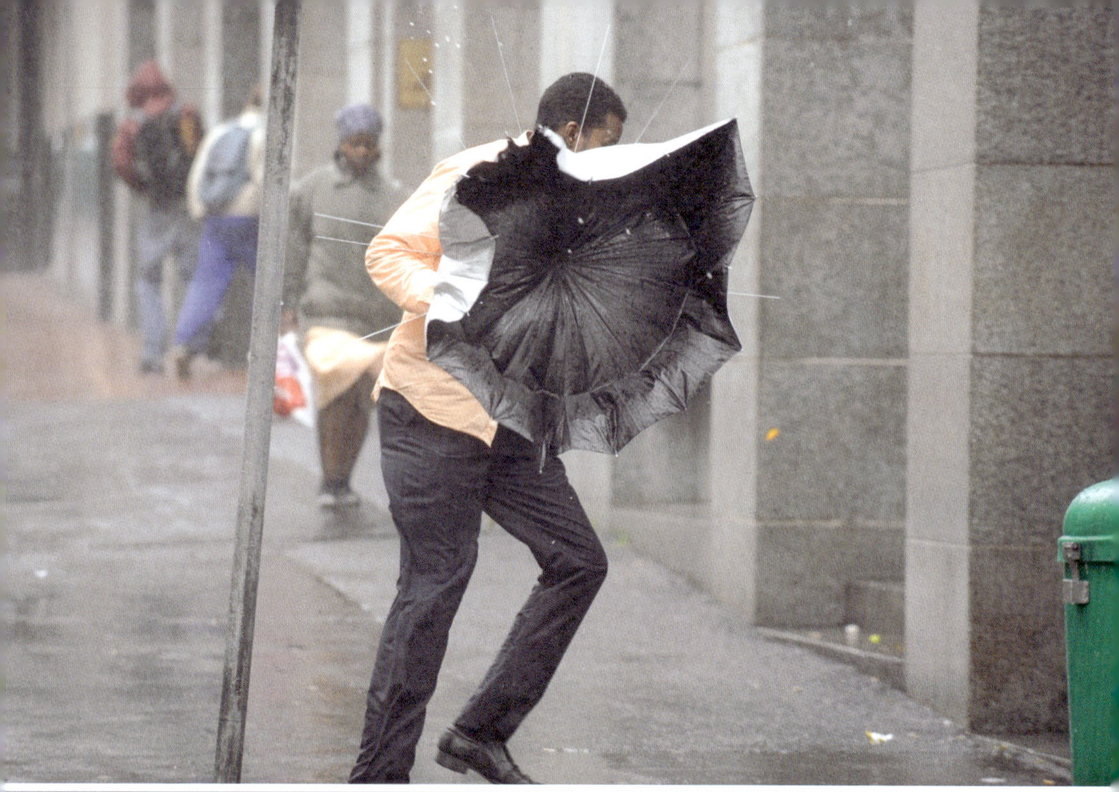

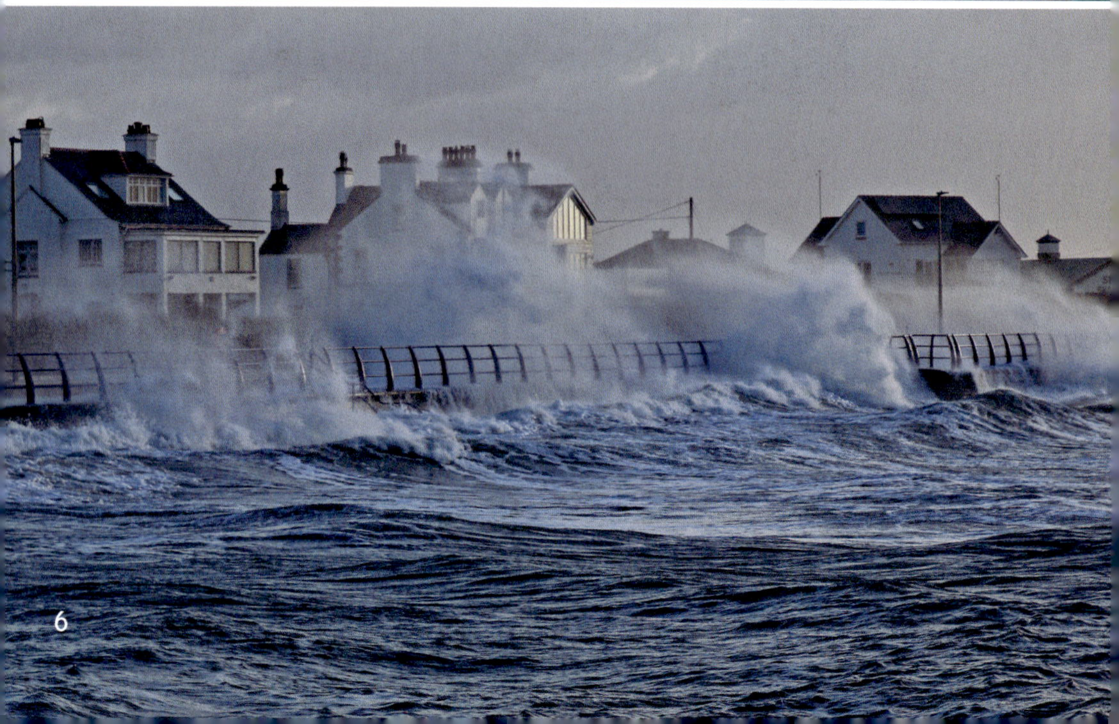

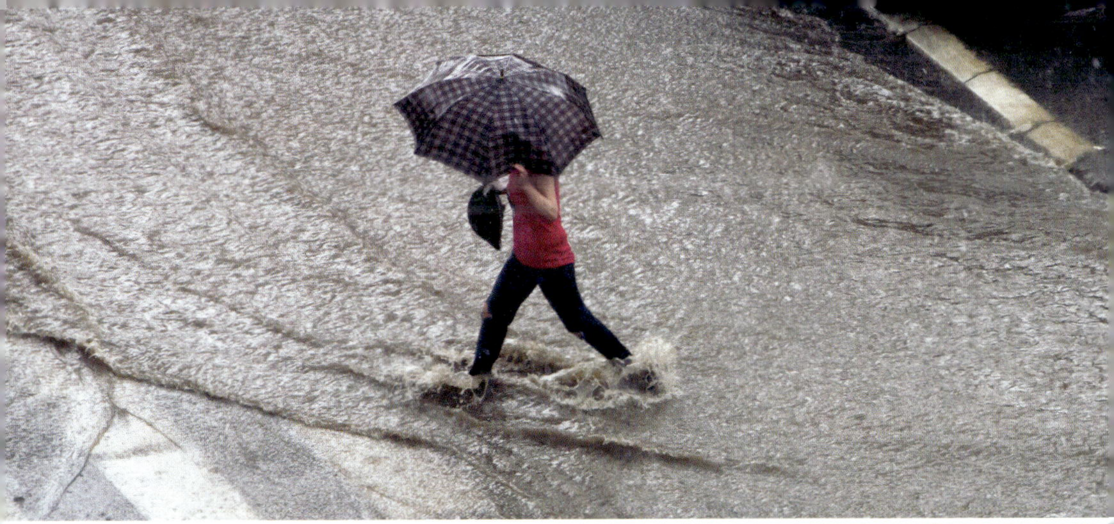

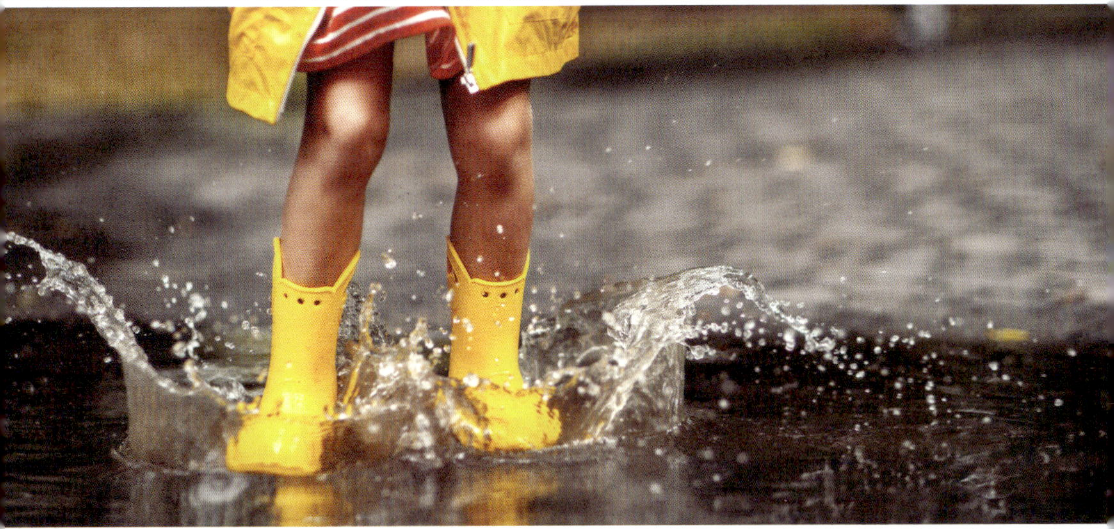

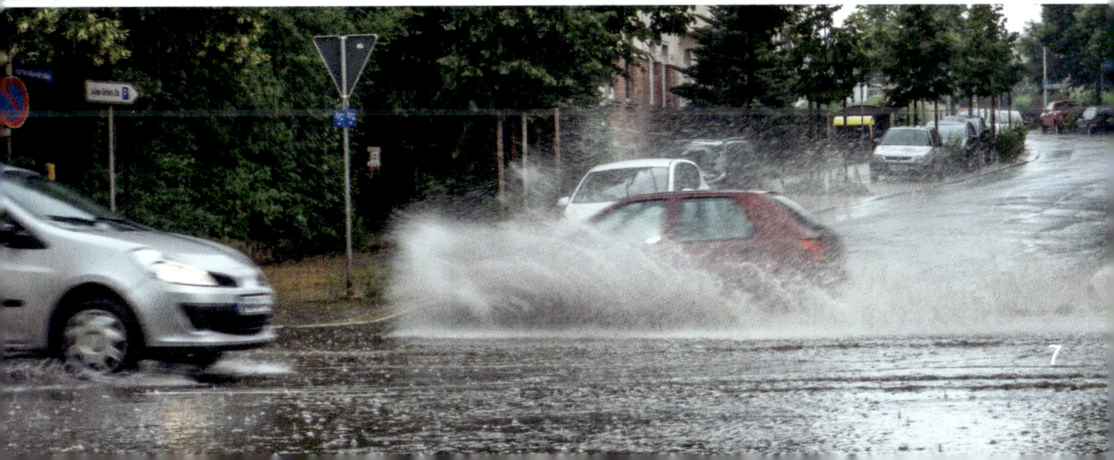

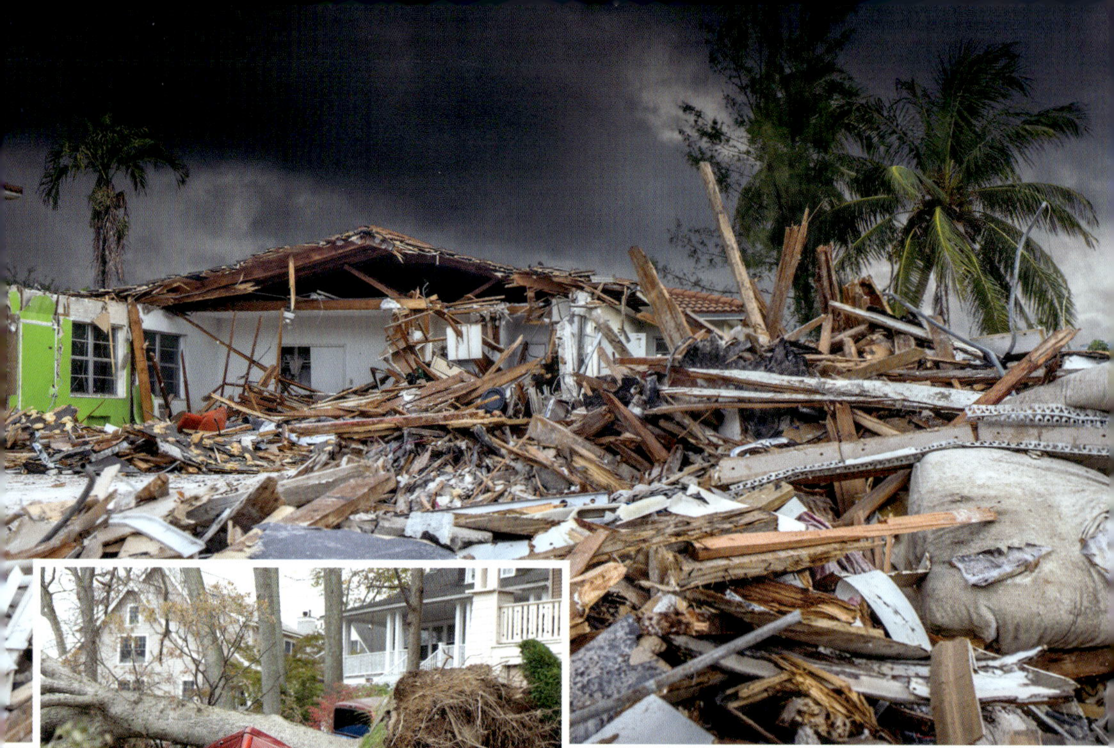
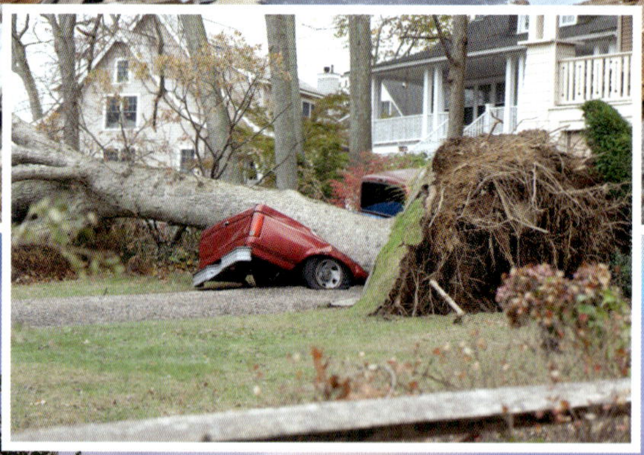
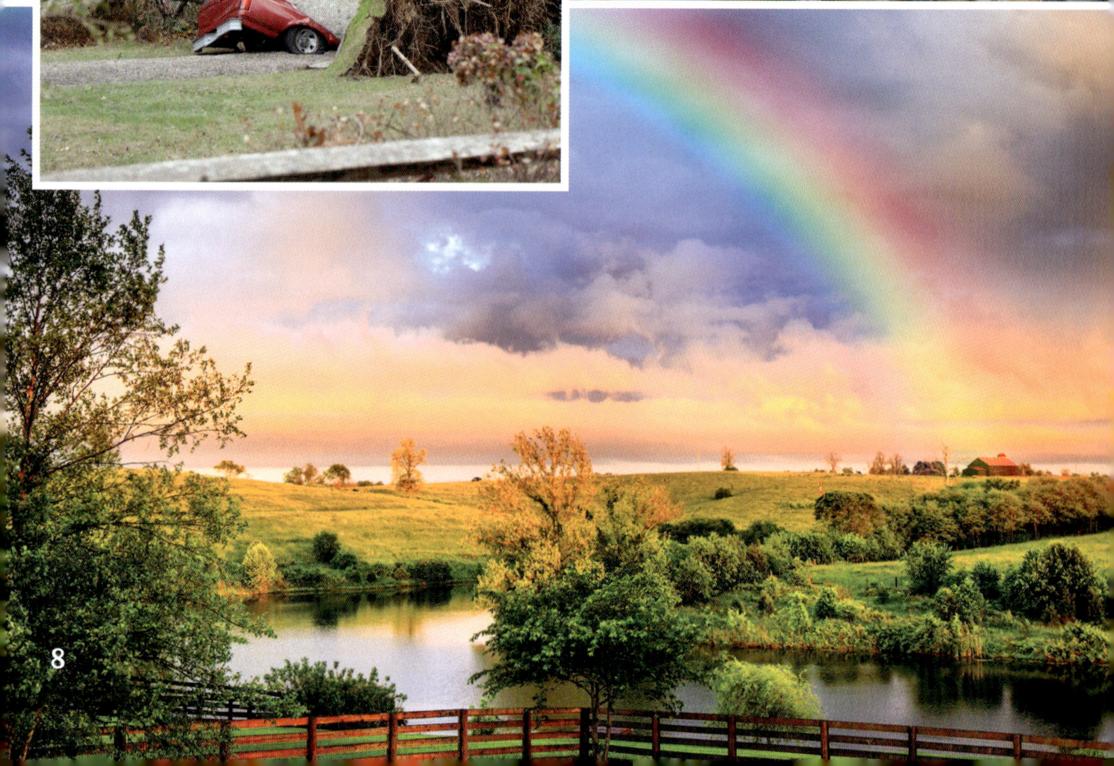